Dedication

For Max, and his Grandad. I love listening to your conversations.

Copyright

©Copyright 2025 Deb Pickering. All Rights Reserved. It is illegal to reproduce, duplicate or transmit any part of this document in either electronic means or printed format. Recording of this publication is strictly prohibited.

Robbie the Robot

Nana and Grandad thought they would introduce 4-year-old Max to their robotic lawn-mower, Robbie. But as soon as Max heard that Robbie was a robot, it created all kinds of thoughts in his head, including ideas about what Robbie might like to eat! Maybe even boys!

My grandad has a robot,
and Robbie is his name.
My grandad thought that chasing
him might be a good new game.

But I didn't want to chase him.
I thought, 'He might eat boys!'

And he moves around the garden,
without making too much noise.

"Grandad, what does he like to eat?"

"Well, he just eats the grass."

I wasn't feeling too convinced,
I moved to let him pass

"Grandad, where are his teeth then?"
"They're underneath his frame,

But he really is a herbivore,
and he's really very tame."

"He's got no eyes!"
"No. No eyes."
"Is that why he's so slow?"

"He's slow because his programme is deciding where to go."

"He could be a transformer and change into a truck!"
I grinned up at my grandad.
That would be a stroke of luck!

My grandad grinned back down at me,
"But then what would I do?
And who would cut my grass for me?
I don't fancy it, do you?"

I sighed, "Not really Grandad. Shall we play the Marble Run?"
"Ok, we'll come back later, when the grass-cutting is done!"

About the Author

Deb Pickering is a nana of 3 gorgeous grandchildren, who lives in York with her husband.
She loves being an active part of the children's lives and says, "They are an absolute inspiration, and better still, they make me laugh, which keeps me young!"

www.ingramcontent.com/pod-product-compliance
Lightning Source LLC
Chambersburg PA
CBHW041120070526
44584CB00002B/228